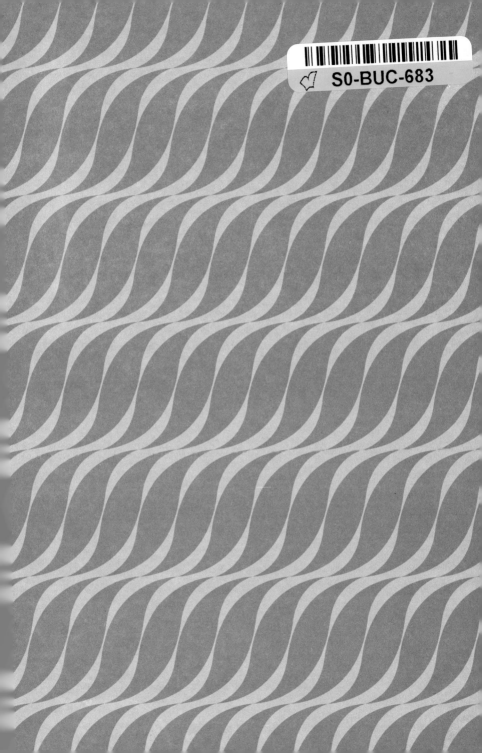

BEST-EVER
BARBECUES

Consulting Editor:
Valerie Ferguson

southwater

Contents

Introduction

There is nothing like the smell of food on the grill for stimulating the appetite—and it's such a fun way to entertain. This book is packed with traditional favorites, as well as some innovative dishes. There are ideas for every course and every occasion.

Meat and poultry have always been barbecue and grill classics, and there are mouthwatering suggestions for steak, ribs, chops and sausages. Shrimp and scallops make quick-cooking kebabs, while fish may be cooked whole or as fillets or steaks. Vegetarians can choose from grilled vegetables, spicy tofu kebabs and even a tasty pizza. And if you have never eaten grilled bananas or other grilled desserts, prepare for a whole new experience.

The introduction offers guidance on choosing and setting up a grill. Safety tips will ensure that your barbecues are hazard-free, healthy and a real pleasure. Recipes for marinades and relishes supplement the many sauces and dips in the individual recipes, and hints and tips offer suggestions to make each barbecue a real feast.

With step-by-step recipes and illustrations, your barbecue is bound to be a success. The only thing this book cannot guarantee is the weather.

Choosing a Grill

There is a wide variety of ready-made grills on the market, and it's important to choose one that suits your needs and the number of people you usually cook for.

Hibachi Grills:

These small cast-iron grills are inexpensive, easy to use and transportable. Lightweight versions are now made in steel or aluminum.

Brazier Grills:

These open grills are suitable for use on a patio or in the yard. Most have legs or wheels, and it's a good idea to check that the height suits you. The cooking area varies in size, and the grill may be round or rectangular. It's useful to choose one that has a shelf attached to the side.

Permanent Grills:

These are a good idea if you often have barbecues at home, as they can be built simply and cheaply. They can be built with ordinary household bricks, but it's best to line the inside with firebricks, which will withstand the heat better. Use a metal shelf for the fuel and a grid at whatever height you choose. Kits containing all you need to build a grill are available.

Kettle Grills:

These have a large, hinged lid that can be used as a windbreak; when closed, the lid lets you use the grill much like an oven.

Gas Grills:

The main advantage of these is their convenience—the heat is instant and easily controllable.

Lighting the Fire

Follow these basic instructions for lighting the fire, unless you have self-igniting charcoal.

1 Spread a layer of aluminum foil on the bottom of the grill, to reflect the heat and make cleaning easier.

2 Spread a layer of fuel on the fire grate about 2 inches deep. Pile the fuel in a small pyramid in the center. Push one or two firelighters into the center, or pour about 3 tablespoons liquid firelighter into the fuel and let sit for 1 minute.

3 Light with a screw of paper or long match and burn for 15 minutes. Spread the coals and let sit for 30–45 minutes, until the coals are covered with a film of gray ash, before cooking.

Types of Fuel

If you have a gas or electric grill, you will not need extra fuel, but most other grills use charcoal or wood.

Lumpwood Charcoal:

This is usually made from softwood, and comes in lumps of varying size. It is easier to ignite than briquettes, but tends to burn up faster.

Coconut–shell Charcoal:

This is not widely available, but makes a good fuel for small grills.

Charcoal Briquettes:

These burn for a long time with a minimum of smell and smoke. They can take time to ignite, however.

Woodchips or Herbs:

These are designed to be added to the fire to impart a pleasant aroma to the food. They can be soaked, to make them last longer. Sprinkle them right on the coals during cooking, or place them on a metal tray under the grill.

Wood:

Hardwoods such as oak, apple, olive and cherry are best for grills, as they burn slowly with a pleasant aroma.

Techniques

Marinating

Marinades add flavor and moisture and are also used to tenderize foods, especially meat. Oil is usually included in a savory marinade; the amount is governed by whether the food is lean or has a relatively high fat content. Arrange the food in a single layer, pour on the marinade and turn the food to coat it evenly.

Basic Marinade

This can be used for meat or fish.

1 garlic clove, crushed
3 tablespoons sunflower or
    olive oil
3 tablespoons dry sherry
1 tablespoon Worcestershire sauce
1 tablespoon dark soy sauce
freshly ground black pepper

Herb Marinade

This is good for fish, meat or poultry.

½ cup dry white wine
¼ cup olive oil
1 tablespoon lemon juice
2 tablespoons finely chopped fresh herbs,
    such as parsley, thyme,
    chives or basil
freshly ground black pepper

Honey Citrus Marinade

This is good for fish or chicken.

finely grated zest and juice of
    ½ lime, ½ lemon and
    ½ small orange
3 tablespoons sunflower oil
2 tablespoons honey
1 tablespoon soy sauce
1 teaspoon Dijon mustard
freshly ground black pepper

Quick Relish

This relish is very easy and quick to prepare and will liven up grilled sausages, burgers and steaks. It has a tangy flavor.

3 tablespoons sweet pickle
1 tablespoon Worcestershire sauce
2 tablespoons ketchup
2 teaspoons prepared mustard
1 tablespoon cider vinegar
2 tablespoons Worcestershire sauce

Cooking in Aluminum Foil

Delicate foods, or foods that are best
if they are cooked in their own juices,
can be cooked in aluminum foil either
on the grill rack or directly in the
coals of the fire with more robust
items, such as potatoes and squash.

1 Cut two pieces of heavy-duty
aluminum foil, making a double layer
large enough to wrap the food. Lightly
grease the foil with melted butter or oil,
then place the food in the center of the
foil and add any flavorings or seasonings.

2 Wrap parcels securely, twisting the
edges of the foil together, so that the
juices cannot escape during cooking.

Safety Tips: Grilling is a
perfectly safe method of cooking if
it's done sensibly—use these simple
guidelines as a basic checklist.
• Make sure the grill is sited on a
firm surface and is stable and level
before lighting. Once lit, do not
move it.
• Keep the grill sheltered from
wind, away from trees and shrubs.
• Always follow the manufacturer's
instructions for your grill.
• Don't try to hasten the fire, and
never pour flammable liquid on to it.
• Keep children (and pets) away
from the fire, and always make sure
the cooking is supervised by adults.
• Keep perishable foods cold until
you're ready to cook.
• Make sure meats such as burgers,
sausages and poultry are thoroughly
cooked—there should be no trace
of pink in the juices.
• Wash your hands after handling
raw meats and before touching
other foods; don't use the same
utensils for raw and cooked foods.
• Have a bucket of sand and a water
spray on hand.
• Trim excess fat from meat and
don't make marinades too oily; fat
can cause dangerous flare-ups.
• Use long-handled barbecue tools
for turning and basting; keep long
oven gloves handy.
• Keep raw foods away from
cooked foods, to prevent possible
cross-contamination.

Charred Artichokes with Lemon Dip

Roasting on a grill is a wonderful way to cook young artichokes.
Finish the dip while the artichokes are cooling slightly.

Serves 4

INGREDIENTS
1 tablespoon lemon juice or white
    wine vinegar
2 globe artichokes, trimmed
1 lemon
12 garlic cloves, unpeeled
6 tablespoons olive oil
sea salt
sprigs of flat-leaf parsley,
    to garnish

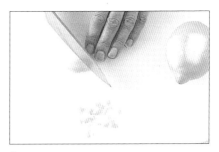

2 Using a sharp knife, thinly pare two strips of lemon zest. Scrape off any pith. Place the zest in a small pan with water to cover. Bring to a boil, then simmer for 5 minutes. Drain, refresh in cold water, then chop roughly. Set it aside. Squeeze the juice and set aside.

1 Add the lemon juice or vinegar to a bowl of cold water. Cut each artichoke lengthwise into wedges. Pull the hairy choke out from the center of each wedge, then drop them into the acidulated water.

3 Drain the artichoke wedges and place in a foil tray or roasting pan with the garlic. Add half the oil and toss to coat. Sprinkle with salt and grill for 15–20 minutes, turning once or twice, until tender and a little charred.

4 Arrange the cooked artichokes on a serving plate and set aside to cool for about 5 minutes. Using the back of a fork, gently flatten the garlic cloves so that the flesh squeezes out of the skins.

5 Transfer the garlic flesh to a bowl, mash into a purée, then add the lemon zest. Using the fork, whisk the remaining olive oil and the lemon juice into the garlic mixture. Serve the artichokes warm with the lemon dip.

Spicy Chicken Wings

These deliciously sticky wings will appeal to adults and children alike, although younger eaters might prefer a little less chili powder.

Serves 4

INGREDIENTS
8 plump chicken wings
2 large garlic cloves, cut into slivers
1 tablespoon olive oil
1 tablespoon paprika
1 teaspoon chili powder
1 teaspoon dried oregano
1 teaspoon salt
1 teaspoon freshly ground black pepper
lime wedges, to serve

1 Using a small sharp knife, make one or two cuts in the skin of each chicken wing and carefully slide a sliver of garlic under the skin. Brush the wings with the olive oil.

2 In a large bowl, stir together the paprika, chili powder, oregano, salt and black pepper. Add the chicken wings and toss together until very lightly coated in the mixture.

3 Barbecue the chicken wings for 15 minutes, until they are cooked through with blackened, crispy skin. Serve with lime wedges.

VARIATION: Chunks of chicken breast and small thighs may also be cooked in this way.

Barbecued Mini Ribs

Ribs are always a favorite. Here they are coated in a rich sauce with just a hint of spice.

Serves 6–8

INGREDIENTS
1 rack of pork ribs,
   about 1½ pounds
6 tablespoons sweet sherry
1 tablespoon tomato paste
1 teaspoon soy sauce
½ teaspoon Tabasco sauce
1 tablespoon light
   brown sugar
2 tablespoons seasoned flour
salt

1 Separate the ribs, then, using a heavy knife, cut each rib in half widthwise to make about 30 pieces.

2 Combine the sherry, tomato paste, soy sauce, Tabasco and sugar in a bowl. Stir in ½ teaspoon salt.

3 Toss the ribs in the seasoned flour in a strong plastic bag, then dip each rib separately in the sherry sauce.

4 Arrange the ribs on the grill rack and cook over hot coals for 30–40 minutes, until cooked through and a little charred. Sprinkle with salt and serve immediately.

VARIATION: Use freshly squeezed orange juice instead of sherry.

Koftas

A fun way to serve lamb. These tasty kebabs are packed with flavors from the Mediterranean.

Serves 4

INGREDIENTS
1¼ cups plain yogurt
¼ cucumber, diced
2 tablespoons fresh mint, finely chopped
salt and freshly ground black pepper
4 cups ground lamb
1½ cups fresh whole-wheat
   bread crumbs
1 onion, grated
1 teaspoon ground cumin
2 garlic cloves, crushed
1 egg, beaten
¼ cup lamb or chicken stock
green salad, to serve

1 To make the yogurt dip, beat the yogurt in a small bowl until smooth. Add the diced cucumber and mint and stir well. Season to taste with salt and freshly ground black pepper. Refrigerate until needed.

2 Place the ground lamb in a bowl and mash thoroughly with a fork to form a fairly smooth paste.

COOK'S TIP: Soak the wooden kebab skewers in cold water for 30 minutes before using to prevent them from burning.

3 Add the bread crumbs and onion. Stir in the ground cumin and garlic. Season well to taste with salt and freshly ground black pepper.

4 Stir in the beaten egg and lamb or chicken stock with a fork. Using your hands, bind the mixture together until it is smooth.

5 Press the meat mixture into short, fat "sausage" shapes by rolling small amounts with lightly floured hands. Line up in rows.

6 Thread the "sausages" onto the prepared wooden skewers (see Cook's Tip) and grill over medium coals for 30 minutes, turning occasionally. Serve the koftas with the yogurt, cucumber and mint dip and a crisp green salad.

Three-color Fish Kebabs

Don't marinate the fish for more than an hour, or the lemon juice will break down the fibers and it will be difficult not to overcook it.

Serves 4

INGREDIENTS
½ cup olive oil
finely grated zest and juice of
    1 large lemon
1 teaspoon crushed chile flakes
12-ounce monkfish fillet, cubed
12-ounce swordfish fillet, cubed
12-ounce thick salmon fillet or
    steak, cubed
2 red, yellow or orange bell peppers, seeded
    and cut into squares
2 tablespoons finely chopped fresh
    flat-leaf parsley
salt and freshly ground black pepper

FOR THE SWEET TOMATO &
CHILI SALSA
8 ounces ripe tomatoes,
    finely chopped
1 garlic clove, crushed
1 fresh red chile, seeded
    and chopped
3 tablespoons extra virgin olive oil
1 tablespoon lemon juice
1 tablespoon finely chopped fresh
    flat-leaf parsley
pinch of sugar

1 Put the oil in a shallow glass or china bowl and add the lemon zest and juice, the chile flakes and pepper to taste. Whisk to combine, then add the fish chunks. Turn to coat evenly.

2 Add the pepper squares, stir, then cover and marinate in a cool place for 1 hour, turning occasionally.

3 Meanwhile, make the salsa by mixing all the ingredients in a bowl and seasoning to taste with salt and pepper. Cover and chill until needed.

4 Thread the fish and peppers onto eight oiled metal skewers, reserving the marinade. Barbecue the skewered fish for 5–8 minutes, turning once. Heat the reserved marinade in a small pan at the side of the grill.

5 Stir the chopped flat-leaf parsley into the heated marinade with salt and freshly ground black pepper to taste. Serve the fish kebabs hot, with the marinade spooned on top, accompanied by the sweet tomato and chili salsa.

VARIATION: Use fresh tuna instead of swordfish if you prefer. It has a similar meaty texture.

Salmon with Herb Marinade

Make the best use of summer herbs in this marinade, which is designed for the grill. Use any combination, depending on your personal taste and what you have to hand.

Serves 4

INGREDIENTS
4 salmon steaks
green salad, to serve

FOR THE MARINADE
fresh herb sprigs, such as chervil,
    thyme, parsley, sage, chives,
    rosemary, oregano
6 tablespoons olive oil
3 tablespoons tarragon vinegar
1 garlic clove, crushed
2 scallions, chopped
salt and freshly ground
    black pepper

2 Mix the chopped herbs with the olive oil, tarragon vinegar, garlic and scallions and season to taste with salt and freshly ground black pepper.

3 Place the fish steaks in a bowl and pour in the prepared herb marinade. Cover with plastic wrap and set in a cool place for 4–6 hours.

1 For the marinade, discard any coarse stems or damaged leaves from the herbs, then chop very finely. You will need two tablespoons for the marinade. Any remaining chopped herbs could be sprinkled on the fish or salad.

VARIATION: This marinade would be equally successful with veal, chicken, pork, lamb or other kinds of firm-fleshed fish.

4 Brush the pieces of fish with the marinade and cook on the grill, turning occasionally, for 5–8 minutes, until they are tender. Brush with the marinade while they cook. Serve with a green salad.

Herbed Trout

The pretty pink flesh and strong flavor of rainbow trout encourages a very simple approach, like this one, when it comes to cooking it.

Serves 4

INGREDIENTS
¼ cup butter, melted
2 teaspoons chopped fresh dill
2 teaspoons chopped fresh
   flat-leaf parsley
4 trout fillets
3–4 tablespoons lemon juice
salt and freshly ground
   black pepper
baby red Swiss chard leaves
   and flat-leaf parsley sprigs,
   to garnish

2 Brush both sides of the fish with the herb butter before placing them in a hinged basket.

3 Grill the fish for 5 minutes on one side, then turn over and cook the other side, basting with the remaining herb butter.

4 Just before serving, sprinkle on the lemon juice. Garnish the trout with Swiss chard leaves and flat-leaf parsley sprigs.

1 Stir together the butter, dill and flat-leaf parsley and season to taste with salt and pepper.

VARIATION: You might like to try substituting cilantro for the dill and flat-leaf parsley used here.

COOK'S TIP: You can also grill whole rainbow trout. Brush with the herb butter as for the fillets, but before placing the fish in a hinged basket, brush the heads and tails with a little water and dip in granular salt to prevent them from burning.

Sea Bass with Fennel, Mustard & Orange

Sea bass is a revelation to anyone unfamiliar with its creamy rich flavor. It has a firm white flesh that goes well with the rich butter sauce.

Serves 2

INGREDIENTS
2 12-ounce sea bass, cleaned and scaled
2 teaspoons Dijon mustard
1 teaspoon fennel seeds
2 tablespoons olive oil
2 ounces watercress
6 ounces mixed lettuce leaves
1 orange, segmented
2 baked potatoes, to serve

FOR THE SAUCE
2 tablespoons frozen orange juice
  concentrate
¾ cup unsalted butter, diced
salt and cayenne pepper

1 For the sauce, place the orange juice concentrate in a bowl and heat over 1 inch boiling water. Remove from heat, and gradually whisk in the butter until creamy. Season to taste, cover and set aside.

2 Slash the bass four times on either side. Combine the mustard and fennel seeds, then spread on both sides of the fish. Moisten with oil and place in a hinged basket. Grill for 12 minutes, turning once.

COOK'S TIP: Potatoes, pricked, brushed with oil and wrapped in foil, can be baked on the grill, but take a long time, and the skin often chars into hard patches.
  An easy alternative is to bake the wrapped potatoes in the oven until nearly done and then finish them on the grill while you are cooking the fish.
  Alternatively, cut into four wedges and parboil in lightly salted water for about 5 minutes. Drain and toss in oil and then cook on the grill for about 15 minutes, turning frequently.

3 Moisten the watercress and lettuce leaves with the remaining olive oil, arrange the fish on two large plates and put the mixed leaves and orange segments to one side. Spoon the orange butter sauce onto the fish and serve with baked potatoes.

Fish Parcels

Sea bass is good for this recipe, but you could also use small whole trout, or white fish fillets, such as cod or haddock.

Serves 4

INGREDIENTS
4 pieces sea bass fillet or 4 cleaned
   whole small sea bass, about
   1 pound each
oil, for brushing
2 shallots, thinly sliced
1 garlic clove, chopped
1 tablespoon capers
6 sun-dried tomatoes, finely chopped
4 black olives, pitted and thinly sliced
grated zest and juice of 1 lemon
1 teaspoon paprika
salt and freshly ground black pepper
crusty bread, to serve
fresh flat-leaf parsley sprigs, to garnish

1 Cut four large squares of double-thick aluminum foil, large enough to enclose the fish. Brush with a little oil.

2 Place a piece of fish in the center of each piece of foil and season well with salt and pepper.

3 Sprinkle on the shallots, garlic, capers, tomatoes, olives and grated lemon zest. Sprinkle with the lemon juice and paprika.

4 Fold the foil over to enclose the fish loosely, sealing the edges firmly so none of the juices can escape. Place on a medium–hot grill and cook for 8–10 minutes. Then open up the parcels and serve with crusty bread, garnished with parsley.

COOK'S TIP: To bake: place on a baking sheet and cook at 400°F for 20 minutes.

Red Snapper with Lavender

Grill with a difference by adding lavender to fresh snapper for a delicious aromatic flavor.

Serves 4

INGREDIENTS

4 red snapper, cleaned and scaled
3 tablespoons fresh lavender flowers or
   1 tablespoon dried lavender flowers,
   roughly chopped
juice and coarsely grated zest of 1 lemon
4 scallions, roughly chopped
¼ cup olive oil
salt and freshly ground black pepper

COOK'S TIP: Sprinkle some
lavender flowers on the hot coals
while cooking the fish.

1 Place the snapper in a large shallow dish. Combine the lavender flowers, lemon juice and zest, scallions and olive oil and season to taste with salt and pepper. Pour onto the fish, cover and set aside to marinate for at least 3 hours.

2 Drain off the marinade and discard the lemon zest. Place the snapper in a hinged basket and cook on a very hot grill for 5–7 minutes on each side, brushing occasionally with the marinade.

Italian Shrimp Skewers

Shrimp are among the most delicious grilled foods.

Serves 4

INGREDIENTS
2 pounds raw jumbo shrimp, peeled
¼ cup olive oil
3 tablespoons vegetable oil
1¼ cups very fine
   dry bread crumbs
1 garlic clove, crushed
1 tablespoon chopped fresh parsley
salt and freshly ground
   black pepper
lemon wedges, to serve

1 Slit the shrimp down their backs and remove the dark vein. Rinse in cold water and pat dry.

2 Put the olive oil and vegetable oil in a large bowl and add the shrimp, mixing them to coat evenly. Add the bread crumbs, garlic and parsley and season with salt and pepper. Toss the shrimp thoroughly, to give them an even coating of bread crumbs. Cover and let marinate for 1 hour.

3 Thread the shrimp onto four metal or wooden skewers, curling them up as you do so, so that the tail is skewered in the middle. Place the skewers on the grill and cook for about 2 minutes on each side, until the bread crumbs are golden. Serve with lemon wedges.

Scallops with Lime Butter

Fresh scallops are quick to cook and ideal for parties. This recipe combines them simply with lime and fennel.

Serves 4

INGREDIENTS
1 head fennel
2 limes
12 large scallops, cleaned
1 egg yolk
6 tablespoons melted butter
oil, for brushing
salt and freshly ground black pepper

1 Trim any feathery leaves from the fennel and reserve them. Slice the rest lengthwise into thin wedges.

2 Cut one lime into wedges. Finely grate the zest and squeeze the juice of the other lime and toss half the juice and zest with the scallops. Season well.

COOK'S TIP: Thread small scallops onto flat skewers, to make them easier to turn.

3 Place the egg yolk and remaining lime zest and juice in a bowl and whisk hard until pale and smooth.

4 Gradually whisk in the melted butter and continue whisking until thick and smooth. Finely chop the reserved fennel leaves and stir them in, with seasoning to taste.

5 Brush the fennel wedges with oil and cook them on a hot grill for 3–4 minutes, turning once.

6 Add the scallops and cook for another 3–4 minutes, turning once, until just cooked but still soft. Transfer to a warm plate and serve immediately with the lime and fennel butter and the lime wedges.

Jerk Chicken

Jerk refers to the blend of herb and spice seasoning rubbed into meat, before it is roasted over charcoal.

Serves 4

INGREDIENTS
8 chicken pieces
vegetable oil, for brushing
salad leaves, to serve

FOR THE MARINADE
1 teaspoon ground allspice
1 teaspoon ground cinnamon
1 teaspoon dried thyme
¼ teaspoon freshly grated nutmeg
2 teaspoons sugar
2 garlic cloves, crushed
1 tablespoon finely chopped onion
1 tablespoon chopped scallion
1 tablespoon wine vinegar
2 tablespoons vegetable oil
1 tablespoon lime juice
1 hot chile pepper, chopped
salt and freshly ground black pepper

2 Place the chicken pieces in a dish and make several lengthwise slits in the flesh. Rub the marinade all over the chicken and into the slits. Cover with plastic wrap and marinate overnight in the refrigerator.

3 When you are ready to cook the chicken, shake off any excess marinade. Brush the chicken with oil and place on the grill. Cook for about 30 minutes, turning often to ensure even browning. Serve the chicken hot with salad.

COOK'S TIP: If you prefer a less spicy marinade, remove and discard the fiery seeds from the chile pepper before mixing with the rest of the marinade ingredients.

1 Combine all the marinade ingredients in a small bowl. Using a fork, mash them together well to form a thick paste.

Chicken with Pica de Gallo Salsa

This dish originates from Mexico. Its hot fruity flavors form the essence of Tex-Mex cooking.

Serves 4

INGREDIENTS
4 chicken breasts
pinch of celery salt and cayenne
   pepper combined
2 tablespoons vegetable oil
cilantro sprigs, to garnish
corn chips, to serve

FOR THE SALSA
10 ounces watermelon
6 ounces cantaloupe
1 small red onion
1–2 green chiles
2 tablespoons lime juice
¼ cup chopped cilantro
pinch of salt

1 First, make the salsa. Remove the rind and as many seeds as you can from the melons. Finely dice the flesh and put it into a bowl.

2 Finely chop the onion, split the chiles (discarding the seeds, which contain most of the heat) and chop. Take care not to touch sensitive skin areas when handling cut chiles. Mix with the melon.

3 Add the lime juice and chopped cilantro, and season with a pinch of salt. Transfer the salsa to a small bowl and set aside in the refrigerator.

4 Slash the chicken breasts deeply to speed up the cooking time. Season the chicken with celery salt and cayenne, and brush with oil. Place on the grill and cook for about 15 minutes, turning frequently.

5 Arrange the chicken on a plate, garnish with cilantro and serve with the salsa and a handful of corn chips.

Turkey Breasts with Tomato-corn Relish

Tasty, economical and quick to cook, turkey breasts are ideal for the grill.

Serves 4

INGREDIENTS
4 skinless boneless turkey breast halves,
    about 6 ounces each
2 tablespoons fresh lemon juice
2 tablespoons olive oil
½ teaspoon ground cumin
½ teaspoon dried oregano
1 teaspoon coarse black pepper
salt
mixed salad leaves, to serve

FOR THE RELISH
1 fresh hot green chile
1 pound tomatoes, seeded and chopped
1½ cups corn kernels, freshly cooked or
    thawed frozen
3 scallions, chopped
1 tablespoon chopped fresh parsley
2 tablespoons chopped cilantro
2 tablespoons fresh lemon juice
3 tablespoons olive oil
1 teaspoon salt

1 With a meat mallet, pound the turkey breasts between two sheets of waxed paper until thin.

COOK'S TIP: Use the cooked turkey, thinly sliced and combined with the relish, as a filling for warmed flour tortillas.

2 In a shallow dish, combine the lemon juice, oil, cumin, oregano and pepper. Add the turkey and turn to coat. Cover and set aside for 2 hours, or refrigerate overnight.

3 For the relish, grill the chile or roast over a gas flame, holding it with tongs, until charred on all sides. When cooled, carefully rub off the skin. For a less hot flavor, discard the seeds. Chop the chile finely and place in a bowl.

4 Add to the chile the remaining relish ingredients and toss well to blend. Set aside.

5 Remove the turkey from the marinade. Season lightly on both sides with salt to taste.

6 Put the turkey breasts on the grill and cook for 2–3 minutes, until browned. Turn and cook on the other side for 3–4 minutes, until it is cooked through. Serve the turkey immediately, accompanied by the tomato relish and salad leaves.

Chicken Kebabs with Tangy Citrus Marinade

Serve on a bed of lettuce leaves and garnish with fresh mint and orange and lemon slices.

Serves 4

INGREDIENTS
4 boneless, skinless chicken breasts
fresh mint sprigs, and orange, lemon or
    lime slices, to garnish (optional)

FOR THE MARINADE
finely grated zest and juice of ½ orange
finely grated zest and juice of ½ small lemon
    or lime
2 tablespoons olive oil
2 tablespoons honey
2 tablespoons chopped fresh mint
¼ teaspoon ground cumin
salt and freshly ground black pepper

1 With a sharp knife, cut the chicken into cubes of about 1 inch.

2 Combine all the marinade ingredients, add the chicken cubes and toss to coat well. Let marinate for at least 2 hours.

3 Thread the chicken pieces onto skewers and barbecue for 15 minutes over low coals on the coolest part of the rack (or raise an adjustable rack). Baste with the marinade and turn frequently. Serve the kebabs garnished with extra mint and citrus slices if desired.

Sausages with Prunes & Bacon

Sausages are always favorite and this is a delicious way to cook them. Serve with crusty bread.

Serves 4

INGREDIENTS
8 large, meaty sausages, such as Toulouse or
    good-quality pork sausages
2 tablespoons Dijon mustard
24 prunes
8 strips bacon

1 With a sharp knife, cut a long slit through one side of each sausage, cutting them about three-quarters of the way through.

2 Spread the cut surface with mustard and then place three prunes in each sausage, pressing them in firmly.

3 Gently stretch the bacon strips out thinly with the back of a round-bladed knife. Wrap around the sausages, securing with toothpicks.

4 Cook the sausages over a hot grill for 15–18 minutes, turning occasionally, until evenly browned and thoroughly cooked.

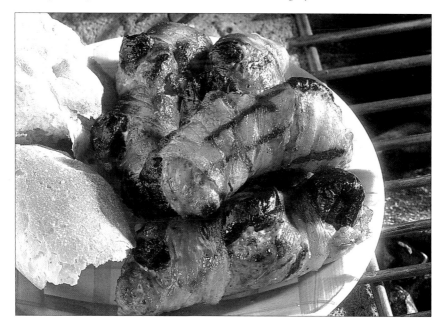

Lamb Kebabs

Kebabs are always a good choice for a barbecue, as they are easy to handle and look very colorful and appetizing.

Serves 6

INGREDIENTS
1½ pounds lean lamb, cut into
   1½-inch cubes
12 shallots or button onions
2 green bell peppers, seeded and cut
   into 12 pieces
12 small tomatoes
12 small mushrooms
rosemary sprigs, to garnish
lemon slices, to garnish
cooked rice and crusty bread, to serve

3 Remove the lamb from the marinade and thread onto six skewers, alternating with the shallots or onions, peppers, tomatoes and mushrooms.

FOR THE MARINADE
juice of 1 lemon
½ cup red wine
1 onion, finely chopped
¼ cup olive oil
½ teaspoon each dried sage and rosemary
salt and freshly ground black pepper

1 For the marinade, combine the lemon juice, red wine, onion, olive oil, herbs and seasoning in a bowl.

2 Stir the cubes of lamb into the marinade. Cover and refrigerate for 2–12 hours, stirring occasionally.

VARIATION: To vary this recipe sprinkle on 2 tablespoons chopped fresh parsley and finely chopped onion, to garnish.

4 Cook the kebabs over the hot coals of a grill for 10–15 minutes, turning them once. Use the leftover marinade to brush onto the kebabs during cooking to prevent the meat from drying out.

5 To serve the kebabs, place them on a bed of freshly cooked rice. Garnish with fresh rosemary and lemon slices and accompany with crusty bread.

Racks of Lamb with Lavender & Balsamic Vinegar

Lavender is an unusual flavoring to use with meat, but its heady, summery scent really works well with grilled lamb.

Serves 4

INGREDIENTS
4 racks of lamb, with 3–4 cutlets each
1 shallot, finely chopped
3 tablespoons chopped fresh lavender
1 tablespoon balsamic vinegar
2 tablespoons olive oil
1 tablespoon lemon juice
salt and freshly ground
   black pepper
handful of lavender sprigs

2 Sprinkle the lavender onto the lamb. Beat together the vinegar, oil and lemon juice and pour them onto the lamb, reserving some of the marinade for basting. Season well with salt and freshly ground pepper, and then turn to coat evenly.

1 Place the racks of lamb in a large bowl or wide dish and sprinkle on the chopped shallot.

VARIATION: Individual lamb cutlets can also be cooked in this way; allow 10–15 minutes, turning occasionally. You can substitute rosemary or thyme for the lavender, if desired.

3 Sprinkle a few lavender sprigs on the coals of a medium-hot grill. Cook the lamb for 15–20 minutes, turning once and basting with any remaining marinade, until golden brown and still slightly pink in the center.

Ground Lamb & Beef Kebabs

In the Middle East, these kebabs are known as *Kabab Kobideh* and are often served with rice stirred with raw egg yolk and melted butter.

Serves 6–8

INGREDIENTS
1 pound lean lamb
1 pound lean beef
1 large onion, grated
2 garlic cloves, crushed
1 tablespoon sumac (optional)
2–3 saffron threads, soaked in
    1 tablespoon boiling water
2 teaspoons baking soda
6–8 tomatoes, halved
1 tablespoon melted butter
salt and freshly ground black pepper
cooked rice, to serve

1 Grind the lamb and beef two or three times until very fine. Place in a large bowl and add the grated onion, garlic, sumac, if using, soaked saffron, baking soda and salt and pepper.

2 Knead by hand until the mixture is very glutinous. It helps to have a bowl of water nearby in which to dip your fingers to keep the meat from sticking.

3 Take a small handful of meat and roll it into a ball. If the ball seems crumbly, knead the mixture in the bowl for a few more minutes.

4 Shape the ball around a flat skewer, molding it around. Repeat with three or four more balls on each skewer, pressing them tightly to prevent the meat from falling off.

5 Carefully thread all of the tomato halves onto two or three separate metal or soaked wooden skewers.

6 When the coals are ready, grill the meat and tomato kebabs for about 10 minutes, basting them with the butter and turning occasionally. Serve on a bed of rice.

COOK'S TIP: Sumac is a favorite Lebanese spice with a slightly sour but fruity flavor. It is available at most Middle Eastern food stores, but it is not essential in this recipe.

Beef & Mushroom Burgers

Nothing compares to the succulence and flavor of homemade burgers. Here, they are flavored with onions, mushrooms and herbs.

Serves 4

INGREDIENTS

1 small onion, chopped
2 cups small cap mushrooms
1 pound lean ground beef
1 cup fresh whole-wheat
    bread crumbs
1 teaspoon dried mixed herbs
1 tablespoon tomato paste
all-purpose flour, for shaping
salt and freshly ground
    black pepper
salad and burger buns or
    pita bread, to serve

1 Place the onion and mushrooms in a food processor and process until finely chopped. Add the beef, bread crumbs, herbs, tomato paste and seasonings. Process for a few seconds, until the mixture binds together but still has some texture.

2 Divide the meat mixture into 8–12 pieces, then press into burger shapes using lightly floured hands.

3 Cook the burgers on a medium grill for 12–15 minutes, turning once, until evenly cooked. Serve with salad, in burger buns or pita bread.

Sizzling Asian Steak

This is a Malaysian method of sizzling meat on a hot grill.

Serves 4–6

INGREDIENTS
4 7-ounce rump steaks
1 garlic clove, crushed
1-inch piece of fresh ginger root,
    finely chopped
2 teaspoons black peppercorns
1 tablespoon sugar
2 tablespoons tamarind sauce
3 tablespoons dark soy sauce
1 tablespoon oyster sauce
vegetable oil, for brushing
carrots and scallions, shredded, to garnish

FOR THE DIPPING SAUCE
⅓ cup beef stock
2 tablespoons ketchup
1 teaspoon chili sauce
juice of 1 lime

1 Place the steaks in a shallow dish. Pound together the garlic, ginger, peppercorns, sugar, tamarind sauce, soy sauce and oyster sauce in a mortar with a pestle. Spoon the marinade onto the steaks, turning to coat thoroughly. Set aside to marinate for up to 8 hours.

2 Scrape the marinade from the meat and place in a pan. Add the stock, ketchup, chili sauce and lime juice and simmer briefly. Keep warm on the side of the grill.

3 Brush the steaks with oil and cook on the grill for 2 minutes on each side, or according to taste. Garnish with the shredded carrots and scallions. Serve the steaks with the dipping sauce.

Mediterranean Vegetables with Marbled Pesto

This is a meal on its own, or delicious served as an accompaniment. Look for baby vegetables, such as baby eggplant and bell peppers.

Serves 4

INGREDIENTS
2 small eggplant
2 large zucchini
1 red bell pepper
1 yellow bell pepper
1 fennel bulb
1 red onion
olive oil, for brushing

FOR THE SAUCE
⅔ cup plain yogurt
3 tablespoons pesto
salt and freshly ground
    black pepper

1 Cut the eggplant into ½-inch thick slices. Sprinkle with salt and let drain in a colander for about 30 minutes. Rinse and dry well with a dish towel or paper towels.

2 Cut the zucchinis in half lengthwise. Cut the peppers in half; remove the seeds but leave the top on. Slice the fennel bulb and the onion into fairly thick wedges.

3 Stir the yogurt and pesto lightly together, to make a marbled sauce. Spoon into a serving bowl.

4 Arrange the vegetables on the hot grill, brush with oil and sprinkle with salt and pepper.

5 Cook the vegetables until golden brown and tender, turning them occasionally. The eggplant and peppers will take 6–8 minutes to cook, the zucchinis, onion and fennel 4–5 minutes. Serve with the marbled pesto sauce.

Herb Polenta with Grilled Tomatoes

Golden polenta with fresh summer herbs and sweet grilled tomatoes is a perfect vegetarian dish.

Serves 4

INGREDIENTS
3 cups stock or water
1 teaspoon salt
1 cup polenta
2 tablespoons butter
5 tablespoons mixed chopped fresh parsley,
  chives and basil, plus extra, to garnish
olive oil, for brushing
4 large plum or beefsteak tomatoes, halved
salt and freshly ground black pepper

1 Prepare the polenta in advance. Place the stock or water in a pan with the salt, bring to a boil, then reduce the heat and stir in the polenta. Stir constantly over medium heat for 5 minutes, until the polenta begins to thicken and come away from the sides of the pan.

2 Remove from heat and stir in the butter, herbs and black pepper.

3 Transfer the mixture to a wide, greased pan or dish and spread it out evenly. Let sit until it is completely cool and set.

4 Turn out the polenta and cut it into squares or stamp out rounds with a large cookie cutter. Brush the slices with olive oil.

COOK'S TIP: Any mixture of fresh herbs can be used, or try using just basil or chives alone, for a really distinctive flavor.

5 Brush the tomatoes with oil and sprinkle with salt and pepper. Cook the tomatoes and polenta on a medium-hot grill for 5 minutes, turning once. Serve garnished with fresh herbs.

Tofu Saté

Grill cubes of smoked tofu until golden and crispy, then serve with a Thai-style peanut sauce.

Serves 4–6

INGREDIENTS
2 7-ounce packages smoked tofu
3 tablespoons light soy sauce
2 teaspoons sesame oil
1 garlic clove, crushed
1 yellow and 1 red bell pepper, seeded
8–12 fresh bay leaves
sunflower oil, for grilling

FOR THE DIPPING SAUCE
2 scallions, finely chopped
2 garlic cloves, crushed
pinch of chili powder or a few drops of
    hot chili sauce
1 teaspoon sugar
1 tablespoon white vinegar
2 tablespoons light soy sauce
3 tablespoons crunchy
    peanut butter

1 Cut the tofu into bite-size cubes and mix with the soy sauce, sesame oil and garlic. Cover and marinate for 20 minutes.

2 Beat the sauce ingredients together until well blended. Avoid using a food processor for this, as the texture should be slightly chunky.

3 Cut the peppers into squares. Drain the tofu and thread the cubes onto 8–12 wooden saté sticks with the pepper squares and bay leaves. Larger leaves may need to be halved.

4 Brush the satés with oil. Cook on the grill, turning the sticks occasionally, until the ingredients are browned and crisp. Serve hot with the dipping sauce.

Eggplant, Tomato & Feta Rolls

Grilled eggplant wrapped around tangy feta cheese, flavored with basil and sun-dried tomatoes, make a wonderfully summery combination.

Serves 4

INGREDIENTS
2 large eggplant
olive oil
10–12 sun-dried tomatoes
    in oil, drained
handful of large, fresh
    basil leaves
5 ounces feta cheese
salt and freshly ground
    black pepper
ciabatta bread, to serve

2 Rinse the eggplant in cold water and dry well. Brush with oil on both sides and grill for 2–3 minutes, turning once, until golden brown and softened.

1 Slice the eggplant lengthwise into ¼-inch thick slices. Sprinkle with salt and layer in a colander. Let drain for about 30 minutes.

VARIATION: Vegans could use tofu in place of the feta. Sprinkle with soy sauce before wrapping.

3 Arrange the sun-dried tomatoes on one end of each eggplant slice and top with the basil leaves. Cut the feta cheese into short sticks and place on top. Season with salt and freshly ground black pepper.

4 Carefully roll the eggplant slices around to enclose the filling. Cook the rolls on the grill for another 2–3 minutes, until they are hot. Serve with ciabatta bread.

Goat Cheese Pizza

Pizzas cooked on the grill are beautifully crisp and golden, which contrasts deliciously with the melt-in-your-mouth topping.

Serves 4

INGREDIENTS
5-ounce package pizza crust mix
olive oil, for brushing
⅔ cup passata
2 tablespoons red pesto sauce
1 small red onion, thinly sliced
8 cherry tomatoes, halved
4 ounces firm goat cheese,
    thinly sliced
handful chopped fresh basil leaves
salt and freshly ground black pepper

1 Mix the pizza dough, according to the package instructions. Roll it out to a circle of about 10 inches in diameter.

2 Brush the dough with oil and place, oiled-side down, on a medium-hot grill. Cook for 6–8 minutes, until firm and golden underneath.

3 Brush the top of the dough with oil and turn the dough over, to cook the other side for 6 minutes.

COOK'S TIP: If the pizza starts to brown too much underneath, raise the grill rack or slip a piece of aluminum foil under the pizza to slow down the cooking.

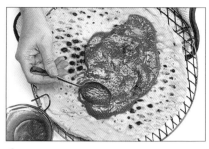

4 Combine the passata and pesto sauce and quickly spread over the cooked side of the crust, to within about ½ inch of the edge.

5 Arrange the sliced onion, halved tomatoes and goat cheese slices on top and sprinkle with salt and freshly ground black pepper.

6 Cook the pizza on the grill for another 8–10 minutes or until the dough has turned golden brown and crisp. Sprinkle with chopped basil leaves and serve.

Spiced Pear & Blueberry Parcels

This combination makes a delicious dessert for a special-occasion party on a summer's evening.

Serves 4

INGREDIENTS
4 firm, ripe pears
2 tablespoons lemon juice
1 tablespoon melted butter
1¼ cups blueberries
¼ cup light brown sugar
freshly ground black pepper

2 Brush the pears thoroughly with lemon juice, to prevent them from turning unattractively brown.

3 Cut four squares of double-thick aluminum foil, each large enough to wrap two pear halves, and brush them with melted butter.

1 Peel the pears thinly. Cut them in half lengthwise. Scoop out the core from each half, with a teaspoon and a sharp knife.

COOK'S TIP: If you wish to assemble the dessert in advance, place a layer of waxed paper inside the parcel, because the acid in the lemon juice may react with the aluminum foil and taint the flavor.

4 Place two pear halves on each piece of foil, with the cut-sides upward. Gather the foil up around the pears, to hold them level.

5 Combine the blueberries and sugar and spoon them on top of the pears.

6 Sprinkle with black pepper. Wrap the foil over and cook on a fairly hot grill for 20–25 minutes.

Apples on Cinnamon Toasts

This simple, scrumptious dessert is best made with a rich bread, such as brioche, but any light, sweet bread will do.

Serves 4

INGREDIENTS
4 apples
juice of ½ lemon
4 individual brioches or muffins
¼ cup melted butter
2 tablespoons light brown sugar
1 teaspoon ground cinnamon
cream or plain yogurt,
    to serve

1 Core the apples and then cut them horizontally in three to four thick slices. Sprinkle with lemon juice.

2 Cut the brioches or muffins into thick slices. Brush with melted butter on both sides.

3 Combine the brown sugar and the ground cinnamon in a small bowl until well combined.

4 Place the apple and brioche slices on the hot grill and cook them for 3–4 minutes, turning once, until they are beginning to turn golden brown.

5 Sprinkle half the cinnamon sugar onto the apple slices and toasts and cook for another minute, until they are a rich golden brown.

6 To serve, arrange the apple slices over the toasts and sprinkle them with the remaining cinnamon sugar. Serve hot, with cream or yogurt.

Bananas with Spicy Vanilla Butter

Bananas are a must for the grill—they're so easy because they cook in their own skins and need no preparation at all.

Serves 4

INGREDIENTS
4 bananas
6 green cardamom pods
1 vanilla bean
finely grated zest of 1 small orange
2 tablespoons brandy or orange juice
¼ cup light brown sugar
3 tablespoons butter
crème fraîche or plain yogurt,
    to serve (optional)

2 Meanwhile, split the cardamom pods and remove the seeds. Crush lightly using a mortar and pestle.

3 Split the vanilla bean lengthwise and scrape out the tiny seeds. Mix with the cardamom seeds, orange zest, brandy or orange juice, sugar and butter, into a thick paste.

1 Place the bananas, in their skins, on the hot grill for 6–8 minutes, turning occasionally, until they turn brownish-black.

4 Slit the skin of each banana, open slightly and spoon in a little of the paste. Serve with a spoonful of crème fraîche or yogurt, if using.

VARIATION: The flavored butter is not essential, but adds extra richness to the bananas. Children may prefer melted chocolate, jam or honey on their bananas.

Oranges in Maple & Cointreau Syrup

This is one of the most delicious ways to eat an orange, and a luxurious way to finish a party.

Serves 4

INGREDIENTS
4 teaspoons butter, plus extra, melted,
    for brushing
4 medium-size oranges
2 tablespoons maple syrup
2 tablespoons Cointreau or Grand
    Marnier liqueur
crème fraîche or fromage frais,
    to serve

1 Cut four squares of double-thick aluminum foil, large enough to wrap the oranges. Brush the center of each with melted butter.

2 Remove some shreds of orange zest, to decorate. Blanch them, dry them and set them aside. Peel the oranges, removing all the white pith and peel and catching any juice that escapes in a bowl.

3 Slice the oranges crosswise into several thick slices. Reassemble them and place each on a square of foil.

4 Tuck the foil up around the oranges, to keep them in shape, leaving the foil open at the top.

5 Combine the reserved orange juice, maple syrup and liqueur and spoon the mixture onto the oranges.

VARIATION: For an alcohol-free version of this dish, omit the liqueur.

6 Add a dab of butter to each parcel and fold over the foil to seal in the juices. Place the parcels on a hot grill for 10–12 minutes, until hot. Serve with crème fraîche or fromage frais, topped with the prepared shreds of orange zest.

This edition published by Southwater

Distributed in the UK by
The Manning Partnership, 251-253 London Road East, Batheaston, Bath BA1 7RL, UK
tel. (0044) 01225 852 727 fax. (0044) 01225 852 852

Distributed in the USA by
Ottenheimer Publishing, 5 Park Center Court, Suite 300, Owing Mills MD 2117-5001, USA
tel. (001) 410 902 9100 fax. (001) 410 902 7210

Distributed in Australia by
Sandstone Publishing, Unit 1, 360 Norton Street, Leichhardt, New South Wales 2040, Australia
tel. (0061) 2 9560 7888 fax. (0061) 2 9560 7488

Distributed in New Zealand by
Five Mile Press NZ, PO Box 33-1071, Takapuna, Auckland 9, New Zealand
tel. (0064) 9 4444 144 fax. (0064) 4444 518

Southwater is an imprint of Anness Publishing Limited

© 2000 Anness Publishing Limited

Publisher: Joanna Lorenz
Editor: Valerie Ferguson
Series Designer: Bobbie Colgate Stone
Designer: Andrew Heath
Editorial Reader: Penelope Goodare
Production Controller: Joanna King

Recipes Contributed by: Catherine Atkinson,
Angela Boggiano, Carla Capalbo,
Lesley Chamberlain, Trisha Davies,
Roz Denny, Nicola Diggins, Joanna Farrow,
Christine France, Silvano Franco, Rosamund
Grant, Deh-Ta Hsiung, Soheila Kimberley, Sue
Maggs, Liz Trigg, Laura Washburn, Steven
Wheeler, Jenni Wright.

Photography: Karl Adamson, Edward Allwright,
James Duncan, Ian Garlick, Michelle Garrett,
Amanda Heywood, Janine Hosegood,
David Jordan, Don Last, William Lingwood,
Patrick McLeavey, Michael Michaels.

A CIP catalogue record for this book
is available from the British Library.

1 3 5 7 9 10 8 6 4 2

Printed and bound in Singapore

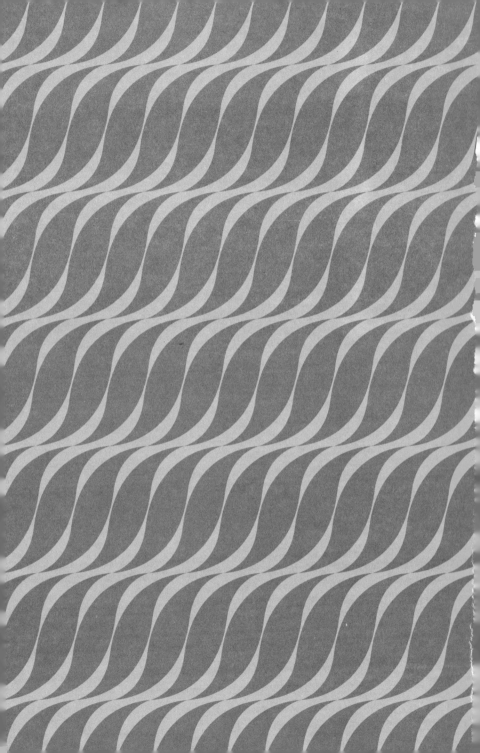